Village Life in England
1860-1940
a photographic record

1 *Previous page* Mother and child at Chideock, Dorset. Photograph by T. A. Colfox and W. Dyson, *c.* 1880s.

2 *Above* Street scene, platinotype by Colonel Joseph Gale, undated.

3 *Overleaf* Cricket match, in central southern England, mid-1930s. Photograph by Eric Guy.

Village Life in England 1860-1940

a photographic record

Jonathan Brown and Sadie B. Ward

B. T. Batsford Ltd · London

ISBN 0 7134 4765 6

Printed in Great Britain by
Butler & Tanner Ltd
Frome, Somerset

for the publishers
B. T. Batsford Ltd
4 Fitzhardinge Street
London W1H 0AH

Contents

Acknowledgements

Most of the photographs in this book have been copied from originals held by the Institute of Agricultural History and Museum of English Rural Life, University of Reading. Where photographs form part of a discrete collection in the Institute, the name of the collection is also given.

General collection: 17–18, 22, 35, 38, 42, 46, 49–50, 55, 58, 60–1, 63, 66, 73, 82, 86, 88, 90, 104, 111, 120, 124–5, 131, 133, 139, 143, 148, 151–2, 155, 157–9, 165, 180–2
P. O. Collier: 19, 98, 109, 150
Council for the Protection of Rural England: 67–8, 137–8, 146–7, 154, 170–9
Farmer and Stock-breeder: 33, 47–8, 57, 77, 99, 127, 129
Farmers' Weekly: 9, 160, 166, 186
Eric Guy: 3, 7, 32, 105, 108, 126, 169
George Long: 95–7
A. J. Pool: 20
Power Farming: 128
John Read: 8, 39, 149
Miss M. Wight: 6, 34, 37, 40, 41, 43, 56, 59, 65, 76, 81, 112–3, 136, 141, 168, 184

The authors and publishers also wish to thank the following organizations and individuals for allowing copies to be made from original photographs or for supplying prints.

Mrs Leila Batchelor (Blackett photos): 10–15
Dr R. J. Esslemont: 110
Mr R. G. Greenaway: 100
Mrs S. Hopson: 51, 87, 118
Mr Chris Howell (an outstanding local history collection, compiled by a Somerset schoolmaster and author): 53–4, 71, 75, 79, 83, 92, 101, 121, 130, 132, 134–5, 153
Mr Lee Irvine: 144
Mrs J. Knock: 64

Mrs Ina Lamb: 89, 106, 164, 185
Mrs Iris Moon (Wilder photos): 23–31, 74, 78, 80, 91, 103, 107, 114–17, 142, 145, 163, 167
Mr C. E. Pady: 16
Mr W. Petch: 183
Mrs C. H. Pope: 2, 4

Dorset County Museum: 1, 21, 85, 102, 123
English Folk Dance and Song Society: 93–4
Goldalming Museum: 44
Hampshire County Museum Service: 122
Hereford City Library: 140
Museum of East Anglian Life, Stowmarket: 36
North of England Open Air Museum: 62
Pitstone Local History Society: 161
John Topham Picture Library: 5
Twyford and Ruscombe Local History Society: 45, 52, 69, 72, 84, 119, 162
Waverley District Museum Service: 70
Wells Museum: 156

The authors wish to thank Mrs Barbara Holden of the Institute of Agricultural History for her valuable assistance with photographs, and the University of Reading Photographic Service for processing all the images contained in this book. They are indebted to Mrs Phyllis Basten for expertly typing the captions, using the latest computer technology. They are particularly grateful to Leila Batchelor, Iris Moon and Christopher Howell for allowing them to use so many of their photographs, and also wish to acknowledge the help of Sadie Down, Ina Lamb, John Finch and John Lockward in the preparation of a number of captions. Information on traditional customs was contributed by Margaret Dean-Smith and Christina Hole. It is, of course, true that any errors are the responsibility of the authors themselves.

Introduction

Between 1860 and 1939 the life of the villages of England changed more than it had done in the previous thousand years of their existence. Villages had been changed before 1860, and sometimes quite radically. People had moved; old villages had died; new villages grown up; new types of farming and trades had been adopted. The difference was that during the period 1860–1939 the village lost its status as a vital component of English provincial life. It became a shadowy appendage to urban England.

The growth of industry from the later eighteenth century onwards drew more of the people of England into the towns. Already by 1860 half the people of England and Wales lived in towns. Fifty years later that proportion was more than four-fifths. People left the country to work in the cities, attracted by the higher earnings in industry. By the mid-nineteenth century this migration was having an appreciable effect on the villages, for population was starting to fall in rural areas, and continued to do so for the rest of the period covered by this book. By the 1880s the shrinking size of England's villages was regarded as a national problem. Surveys were made of the 'drift from the land', expressing concern that the nation's vitality was being drained away to the towns so that the villages were left with the 'one-eyed, the lame, deaf, weaklings, the small and half wits', as one farmer complained in 1902, with perhaps a little exaggeration. But neither the analysis of the problem, nor such schemes as county council allotments and smallholdings could stem the tide: there simply were not the opportunities in the village to match those of the town.

The isolation of the village was broken down during this period. Again, this was a process that had

4 Village pond, platinotype by Colonel Joseph Gale, undated.

5 Children at Northiam, East Sussex, *c. 1900*.

started long before 1860, with the improvements to transport brought about by turnpike roads and canals. Railways, and later, motor cars and lorries, increased the pace of this change, by turning into hours journeys that had taken days. The trains could take the produce of the village more quickly and efficiently to distant towns, and this was a great boon to some people. Dairy farming, for instance, was able to expand because fresh milk could be delivered daily to towns as far as a hundred miles away. But as much traffic came the other way. The railways brought cheap manufactured goods from towns across the country. Pottery came from Staffordshire, pots and pans from Birmingham, furniture from London. Even the fabric of the village could be changed as new cottages were built of bricks delivered by train from Peterborough. It was not only that the town-made goods were cheap. The closer and more rapid communications between town and village brought by railways, newspapers and the penny post made country people more aware of what was going on in the towns, and keener to follow urban fashions.

The effect of these changes on the economic balance of the village was quite drastic. The old trades and crafts of the country were either killed or seriously weakened. In 1860 wheelwrights, blacksmiths, millers, shoemakers, carpenters, hurdlemakers, and a great range of other tradesmen were to be found in the villages of England. Several depended on agriculture for their livelihood, and in the 1860s farming was prosperous and provided plenty of work. Implements, from scythes and rakes to ploughs and wagons, needed repairs. Hurdles were needed to confine the sheep. The farm horses needed shoeing. A large village might contain a considerable diversity of trades, with perhaps two or three millers as well as shopkeepers, shoemakers and the like. In a small village there could be only a handful of tradesmen, but their prosperity was vital to the health of the community.

From the 1870s on, the markets for village trades

8

began to contract. Farming descended into a depression in which it generally continued, except for the years of the First World War, down to 1939. The farmers' custom was now harder to come by, while the decline of village populations reduced the size of the craftsmen's market. And the influx of factory-made goods from the towns cut the ground from under the village trades. By 1939 nearly all the craftsmen had gone. A few new trades had arisen: there was a garage in many villages, often in the proprietorship of a former blacksmith or wheelwright. But these did not adequately fill the gap left by the old crafts.

The departure of the young to work in towns, and the demise of old trades upset the composition of the village. The upper end of the social scale was also disrupted as old gentry families began to leave the village. Some were doing so at the end of the nineteenth century as depression in agriculture reduced the income from their land. But bigger changes at the halls and manor houses came just after the First World War. Landowners cashed in on a temporary rise in the value of land, and estates were broken up wholesale. Between 1918 and 1921 about 6 million acres of agricultural land in England and Wales changed hands, nearly all of that being sales from great estates. The break-up of estates and the departure of the old families had a profound effect on the spirit of the village, for the big house with its band of estate workers had given an order to the parish that was not easily replaced. The First World War created yet bigger gaps in village society through the loss of many of its young men. Almost all who were fit to serve joined the forces, amounting to as much as a quarter of the village's population. Often more than a third of that number, sometimes nearly half, were killed in action.

New people did come to the villages, at least to those that were reasonably accessible from the towns. But the newcomers changed the character of village society, for they brought more of the urban tastes and attitudes into the countryside. Some of the squires were replaced by wealthy businessmen (like the sauce manufacturer who had bought the hall in Richmal Crompton's *William* stories!). Other middle-class people from the towns retired to the village, or else travelled daily to their offices in the city. A few new professional people came to live and

6 Church in Herefordshire, 1930s. Photograph by Miss M. Wight.

work in the village, for example the policeman or the college-trained schoolteacher. And there were the working-class people who moved to the overspill estates built in the countryside. Between 1912 and 1939 about 862,500 houses were built in rural areas for the overflowing populations of London and other great cities. Local authorities provided 162,500 of these, private builders the remainder. Again, the people who moved into these houses mostly worked outside the village. The estates were usually sited in places near a provincial town where the newcomers could find work.

The increase in the number of people living in the village and working in a town was made possible by improvements in transport. In 1860 the principal means of transport for the majority of the village population was walking, and there were plenty of labourers who walked regularly five miles or so to work on a farm in the next parish, in a quarry outside the village, or to a nearby town. There might be

7 Driving cows, Teffont Evias, Wiltshire, 1930s.
Photograph by Eric Guy.

railway branch lines, but for the village labourers in the nineteenth century the train was often little help. As Edwin Grey observed of the journey from his village of Harpenden to the town of St Albans, the train fare was more than the cottagers could afford. Besides, they said, by the time they had walked to Harpenden station and then from St Albans station to the town centre they could be half way down the road from their cottages to the town, so they might as well walk all the way.

A real difference was made to rural transport by the bicycle. The invention of the chain-driven safety bicycle with pneumatic tyres in the 1880s gave rural workers much greater freedom to travel. Again, for most, the distance covered would be no more than five or six miles, although the more robust might regularly pedal ten miles or so to work. But even the five miles were covered more quickly, so that it was a little less of a struggle to reach the works in town at 6

a.m. After the First World War, the number of rural bus services grew considerably, providing yet more opportunities for travel to work. The ownership of cars also increased rapidly during the interwar years. Before 1914 motoring in the country was generally confined to the hardy, the enthusiastic, and the rich, although the beginnings of mass production were already bringing cars within the range of such people as the village doctor. After the war the revolution in car production brought their cost down by more than half between the early 1920s and mid-1930s. The number of cars in Great Britain increased from 245,882 in 1921 to just under two million in 1938 as more of the middle class of both town and country took to the road.

The town was brought out to the village again with the development of tourism, which began to reach the countryside in the 1870s. 'Every year', wrote Richard Jefferies in *The Globe* in 1877, 'a large number of pleasure seekers, who have grown tired of the bustling cities by the sea, who have exhausted Brighton and Scarborough, and a host of similar places, endeavour to get out of the beaten track of holiday-making, and to discover some quiet spot where they may really rest awhile.' He went on, in this article and in a number of others, to recommend the pleasures of 'village hunting', and offered suggestions as to places quite accessible by railway excursions. Many took the advice of Jefferies and other writers. Touring in the countryside became more popular with cycling, which was much in vogue at the turn of the century. But the great boom in rural recreation followed the First World War as the craze for fresh air grew, and as motor cars and charabancs took people cheaply and speedily for day trips and holidays round England's villages. New organizations were set up to cater for the out-of-doors enthusiasts. The Youth Hostels Association was founded in 1931, the Ramblers' Association in 1934, while the Cyclist's Touring Club and the Camping Club were older, dating from 1883 and 1906.

Tourism both brought new opportunities and placed new demands on countrymen. There were opportunities in catering for the visitors' needs. Inns providing for cyclists appeared at the end of the nineteenth century, to be followed by garages, tea shops, and gift shops. All of this brought money into the village, but the influx of townsmen placed pressures upon the village. The visitors expected the village to live up to idyllic conceptions of the countryside: to be full of rustic charm, with thatched cottages, rambling roses and the like. They expected unhindered access to every square inch of the country. They expected to be able to leave their cars and buses anywhere they pleased while they went for a tramp in the woods. Though they might go some way towards meeting such demands, the villagers also built up a hearty resentment of the townsmen and their apparently careless attitude towards country ways and manners. Hedges began to sprout 'No Trespassing' signs, footpaths were lined with barbed wire, and some fairly polemical literature was published debating the rights and responsibilities of ramblers.

This half welcoming, half resentful attitude to tourists had its equivalent in other aspects of the relationship between town and country. Villagers frequently remained extremely suspicious of the towns and their way of life. Townspeople were regarded as showy, pretentious and shallow, always flaunting their wealth. The people who moved into the country from the towns were treated with similar caution, while some of the newcomers behaved snobbishly enough to confirm all the old villagers' suspicions. Yet at the same time country people were envious of the higher standard of living of the towns, and wanted to emulate it. They welcomed the comforts which factory-made goods brought to the cottage: such things as easy chairs, packaged foods and stainless-steel cutlery. There was likewise much that was attractive about urban fashions and culture. Writers like William Cobbett in the 1820s, and others before him, had complained that country people were abandoning their traditional ways of life. The difference between earlier ages and this one was that now the infusion of a new culture was more rapid and more complete. The spread of the new ways was helped by swifter national means of communication. In the 1860s almost the only newspapers to be found in village homes, and then only in the better-off ones, were the local papers, full of information about meetings of local agricultural societies, accidents and injuries happening with threshing machines, and reports of local markets. By 1914 national newspapers, especially the popular ones like the *Daily Mail*, were read in most village households. They, through their news and advertisements, brought metropolitan fashions to the attention of country people. Between the wars this trend was taken further as shopping by mail-order catalogue spread into the villages. By 1939 there was the radio as well, although not possessed by every home; but for those without, the pub might have one for all to hear.

In a number of ways village life became more tamed and domesticated. The administration of the country was tidied up with the creation of new county and rural district councils. The establishment of county constabularies brought a new regime of law and order. For some, the policeman represented an imposition of middle-class, urban respectability, and was consequently distrusted by the older members of the village. 'There is probably no lonelier man in the parish than the constable', wrote George Sturt. 'Of course he meets with civility, but his company is avoided.' Not all shared such a view. Edwin Grey remembered '"George Best the Bobby" ... would, as he perambulated the various parts of

8 Cottage at Arlington Row, Bibury, Gloucestershire, 1920s. Photograph by John Read.

his wide and scattered parish, be met with many a cheery greeting, not much sign of fear being evinced.'

The spread of urban tastes and respectability had its influence on the cultural and social activities of the village. The traditional pastimes, folk dancing, mumming, and the like, began to seem old fashioned and uncouth. People turned from them to activities which were more disciplined, and like those of the town. Football matches changed from being a general mêlée into fixtures organized by a village club and played according to the rules of the Football Association. Clubs and societies were founded for other activities ranging from cricket to amateur dramatics. The gentry and middle-class leaders of village society tended to encourage such clubs as preferable to the old festivities which they were apt to regard as excuses for drunkenness. The hall and rectory were often especially influential in the foundation of the Women's Institute which became one of the most important organizations in the village. A new focal point for social activities was provided by village halls. A few were built early in the twentieth century, but most came after the First World War. Improved transport also had its effect on social life, especially after 1918; the young could take new opportunities to visit the market town where they could go to the cinema, or maybe a dance hall, where a band playing passably like Henry Hall would be much preferred to the jigs and reels of old village folk musicians.

The appearance of the village changed during these years to a considerable extent as a result of some of the developments already mentioned. The need for better cottages was recognized in the mid-nineteenth century, and during the 1850s and 1860s landowners were building new houses for the labourers in an effort to stem the flow of able-bodied workers away from the villages. In this last aim the new cottages were unsuccessful, but they did provide far better accommodation than the various forms of timber-framed and cob-walled building of older cottages. Agricultural depression reduced the rate of new building to a trickle until after the First World War when the new overspill estates, the council houses for farm workers and the villas for the middle classes, were all built in quite large numbers. These represented further improvements in accommodation, with amenities such as gas, electricity, and, in a few villages, water, being available by the 1930s. Yet the new estates and villas created a certain amount of contention, as their styles and their use of materials at variance with local tradition began to impart a suburban appearance to country districts.

These changes in village life did not affect all places equally. Accessibility was one reason for this. The isolated villages were less likely to be influenced by tourism, and urban fashions and values. But the isolated villages were also most likely to lose population. The old way of life might carry on in such a village, but with little new vitality to sustain it. Elsewhere there might be more thriving survivals of village life, especially where a fairly strong element of paternalistic leadership continued from the hall, the rectory, or large farms. There were also revival movements trying to maintain strong rural traditions in economic and social activities. The Rural Industries Bureau was established with the aim of maintaining the old craftsmanship of the countryside and adapting those skills to twentieth-century needs. The Council for the Preservation of Rural England sought to prevent the unthinking destruction of the country by townsmen, and campaigned vigorously, for instance, for planning controls which would prevent unsympathetic red-tiled roofs from appearing in Cotswold stone villages. The folk revival got under way at the end of the nineteenth century, and was given organized form in the English Folk Dance and Song Society, the Morris Ring, and other associations. But movements for revival and conservation had inevitably a certain artificiality about them, and were in any case often inspired by people of the towns rather than the country.

Although the village was being swamped by the new urban culture, it cannot be said to have been all loss. Villagers made important gains, especially in material comforts. Better houses, furnishings, food, clothing, and dozens of other products of modern industry came their way. Improved communications and transport meant villagers could not only hear more of the outside world, but could go and see it. Besides that, by breaking down the old isolation these changes made villages part of the outside world. In some respects that gave the village a new sense of identity, for the attractiveness of the village environment and the closeness of much of village life came to be more appreciated as things worth having. Despite the loss of so much of its old farming population, the village was able to survive intact to face the challenge of the post-war era.

14

9 Bowland bridge, on the boundary between Lancashire and Westmorland, 1940s.

Note on the Commentaries

Jonathan Brown contributed the commentaries on Work, Shops and markets, Domestic life, Church and chapel, and Communications.

Sadie Ward contributed the other commentaries.

Places are located within the county boundaries which existed at the time of photography, and in the text no account has been taken of the local government reorganization of 1974. In some photographs the place is unidentified but all the pictures are believed to have been taken in England. The book does not attempt to cover Scotland and Wales. A considerable number of photographs is precisely dated; in other cases an approximate estimate of the date has been established from internal evidence.

The Traditional Community

The village often lay within the penumbra of a landed family, which still had wealth enough to live in the grand manner and whose easy assumption of the privileges of rank and birth was balanced by a long tradition of unpaid service to the community. This ethos is reflected in a poem composed by a housemaid about the Blackett family of Thorpe Lea House, near Windsor, Berkshire, in the late nineteenth century; verses from it have been used to accompany photographs 10–15 taken from a Blackett family album, c. 1880s.

10 Thorpe Lea House.

'Tis a large white house three storeys high,
The grounds and park spread far and near,
And from one year's end to another, it does
Lofty and stately appear.'

11 The drawing room.

'All the furniture in the house
Is costly, choice and good,
And most of the oil paintings and pictures
Are framed with old oak and rosewood.'

12 The Blackett family, with 'Papa' wearing top hat, far left.

'Mr and Mrs Blackett are
The host and hostess of Thorpe Lea,
And more real gentry anywhere,
I'm sure you'll never see.'

13 The establishment required considerable staff, including the kitchen gardeners seen here.

'There's the coachman, groom, and stable-boy,
Gardeners not less than five,
When they're all at work together,
The place looks quite alive.'

14 & 15 The Blacketts also took a lead in local charity work, providing a tea for the aged poor from the 'Union' or local workhouse.

'They are known and respected for miles round
By the rich, the trades-people, and poor,
The latter, often, who greatly need help,
From Thorpe Lea relief procure.'

If the principal landowner stood at the head of the local community, farmers, rightly perhaps, considered that they constituted its backbone. As a class they were conservative and patriotic, tending to uphold the 'natural' order of things, and as befitted important local employers, they took an active part in parish affairs.

16 Tenant farmers, spring 1900. The photograph shows Jacob Pady with his second wife Ellen (both seated) and children from his two marriages. He and his sons farmed Whitwell farm (160 acres) at Colyford, east Devon, as a tenant of Sir William Pole of Shute. On horseback in the uniform of the Devon Yeomanry is John Pady, aged 21.

17 The position of farm workers, although still grim, improved slowly from the mid-nineteenth century as many left the land. Even so, it is doubtful if the man pulling old thatch into the tip cart is really a labourer. His appearance, with clean white shirt and sturdy leather boots, suggests that he is the farmer posing for the camera. Neither is this surprising, as the photograph is an early one, taken in Devon in the late 1850s.

18 *Above* The Church of England produced many outstanding parsons in the late nineteenth century. Not all filled the conventional mode or upheld the establishment. The photograph shows the Reverend John Whitmore Black, the rector of Launcells in Cornwall, about 1900. He was a scholar, radical thinker and a follower of Henry George (an American who considered that landlordism lay at the root of all social ills and advocated that land rent be taxed to extinction; the revenue would pay for social reform, including old-age pensions). Black was rector of Launcells for 41 years and, despite his advanced views on religion and politics, died a much loved and respected local patriarch.

19 *Above right* The inn remained one of the focal points of village life. It provided a meeting place and cheap entertainment, and men could relax there after work. The photograph shows the landlord, James Pullen, at the door of the Greyhound Inn at Tidmarsh, Berkshire in 1909. Note the blurred image of the hens in the roadway. Photograph by P. O. Collier.

20 *Right* After about 1860 the provision of shops in rural areas increased greatly. Even quite small villages would have a general shop like the one shown here at Chipstable, Somerset. Village shopkeeping was frequently carried on by women to supplement their husbands' incomes or to maintain some small independence after being widowed. This grocer's shop was open for only part of the week and was run by Mrs Sydney Smith, whose husband was employed by W. H. Pool. The Pool family farmed about 60 acres in the locality as well as running a small engineering works and this store. The photograph was taken by William Henry's son, Alfred, who described himself in the 1906 edition of Kelly's Somerset Directory as a 'photographic artist'.

21 *Above* Dorset labourer, probably 1890s. The man's occupation is unknown, although his spade and long leather gaiters suggest that he may have been ditching, a task usually undertaken during the long winter months, when there was less to do on the land.

22 'A Wayfarer', *Country Life*, 17 September 1904. Those unable to find work sometimes took to the open road and a life of vagrancy. In the article accompanying the photograph shown below, the author noted the reality of such an existence.

'During one of the wettest days of last month the writer pulled up beside a party of two who had made a fire, and, despite the rain, were cooking their victuals by the wayside. He thought them two miserable wretches. They were quite young, a man and a woman, neither of them more than twenty-five, and their ruddy skins proclaimed them true children of the open air; but all the pot they had was an old mustard tin, and its contents a piece of fat bacon stolen or begged at some wayside house, with a couple of duck's eggs, the proceeds of theft, one may well imagine . . . . So much for actuality as opposed to romance.'

Sulham Estate and Village

The photographs presented here (23–31) are from albums belonging to Mrs Iris Moon, whose family (the Wilders) have held land in Sulham since the early fifteenth century. They were taken by Henry Beaufoy Wilder (until his death in 1908) and then by his son, Henry Charles Wilder. Both were keen amateur photographers and their work provides a valuable record of Sulham—the estate and village community—during three decades of social change.

23 The Wilder family, taken outside the porch of Sulham house, *c.* 1907. Henry Beaufoy Wilder is standing, second from left in the back row. An energetic man, he combined the rôles of rector of Sulham, trustee of the manor and village doctor. He was also interested in the mechanical arts, having purchased one of the first cars in Berkshire, a Benz Vélo, in the mid-1890s. He installed an electric lighting plant, using a stationary steam engine to generate power for this and other gadgets, and had a fully equipped photographic studio—known as the crystal palace—on the second floor of his workshop in Sulham rectory. His eldest son, Henry Charles, is shown in clerical garb on the right of the photograph.

24 Sulham rectory, *c*. 1900. Note the tennis court in the foreground—an addition to many large houses with spacious grounds in the last two decades of the nineteenth century. The siting of the court here, on rather wet ground, often caused difficulties for the players. ·

25 *Opposite, above* Sulham farm, September 1884. One of eight farms on the 1720 acre estate, it comprised about 200 acres. Many of the wooden objects depicted here—the wheelbarrow, ladder, basket and besom—may have been produced from estate coppice. Coppice was the term given to planted woodland, harvested periodically every eight to twenty years, according to species. The system of coppicing, with standard or mature trees grown for timber, was maintained at Sulham until it became uneconomic in the interwar period.

27 *Above* Hay harvest, *c.* 1885. After the hay is cut and completely dry, it is raked into windrows, as here, before loading into a wagon. The woman, second from left, is wearing a sun bonnet as protection against the heat; her younger companion has opted for a more modern form of headgear.

26 Timber yard at the sawmill, June 1885. The sawpit, where the trees were cut into usable lengths, is shown on the left.

29 *Below* Mr and Mrs Spackman, 1890s. Nothing is known about this couple, although their demeanour indicates that life has not been easy for them. Mr Spackman wears a high-necked waistcoat, corduroys and check shirt with straight-set sleeves, loose cut for ease of movement. A neatly-tied kerchief and wide-brimmed felt hat add a touch of distinction to his otherwise shabby outfit. His wife is wearing a closely pinned shawl, over a cotton dress, with no doubt several petticoats underneath. A sun bonnet provides the necessary headgear. It is interesting to note that Mrs Spackman is not wearing a wedding ring; what was the reason for its absence?

28 *Above* Two young estate workers, mid-1890s. The boy on the right is wearing a short jacket and trousers of corduroy (the most usual material for rural work clothes at this time), while his brother is wearing a similar outfit of much frayed and repaired cloth. Both are wearing conventional soft caps and scarves to complete their working class 'uniform'.

30 Mrs Mortlock, aged 97, taken about 1908. This remarkable old lady would have been born during the Napoleonic Wars. She wears a colourful paisley-design blouse, with kerchief, over a full skirt. Her long white apron, characteristic of rural 'peasant' dress, suggests that she is still able to do a few household chores, while the close-fitting ruched cap, is clearly a favourite.

31 Photographer at work: Henry Beaufoy Wilder, mid-1890s.

Work

The land

Farming was the means of livelihood for most villagers during the 80 years covered by this book. However, the nature of the work changed dramatically, and the numbers working on the land declined, as more machinery was introduced, and as farmers tried to cut their labour bills to meet falling prices for their produce.

32 Plough teams either setting out or returning from work in the village of Hampnett, Gloucestershire, in 1935. Although farmers were by now using more tractors, the horse remained the main form of motive power on the land throughout this period. Photograph by Eric Guy.

33 Dairying became a more important branch of farming during these years, especially for the sale of liquid milk, as its price remained quite stable while cereals and meat prices fell. Dairying also changed greatly during the interwar years to meet stricter demands for hygiene. Here bottled milk is being loaded into a sterilizer at a farm in Penkridge, Staffordshire, in 1935.

34 Growing hops was one of the more specialized branches of farming, and one which brought the town to meet the country, as townspeople came out to work as hop pickers. This photograph of 1934 shows the hops being picked and put into the bin or basket. It was not hard work, but very time-consuming since it took thousands of hops to fill a bin. It could also be tiring, since despite the impression given by this posed photograph by Miss M. Wight, most of the work would be done standing up.

Village industry

35 One of the less usual jobs for the blacksmith by 1879, when this photograph was taken, was shoeing oxen. It was also a labour-intensive task as the ox required more restraining than a horse would. Taken at Saddlecombe, near Brighton; the Sussex Downs were one of the areas where oxen were still used in farmwork.

36 The more conventional range of the blacksmith's work is illustrated in this view of a forge in Suffolk. There was the repair of farm implements and domestic utensils besides, for those qualified, farriery work.

37 The wheelwright's was a traditional craft already undergoing changes by the end of the nineteenth century as a result of competition from the standard factory-made wagons and carts. Although declining in numbers, wheelwrights did continue in business in some villages until the end of the period. This one is at work at Fawley, Herefordshire, in 1937. Photograph by Miss M. Wight.

39 *Below* Baskets for farm and domestic use were always in demand, and not a few villages had a basketmaker amongst their tradesmen, although most were based in the market towns. This woman is making a frail or flail, a basket made of rush. It was a type of basket often used by the farm labourer to take his mid-day meal of bread and cheese out to the fields. Photograph by John Read.

38 *Above* The boot and shoemaker was one of the tradesmen more frequently found in villages, a reflection of rough ill-surfaced roads, and the amount of work that required heavy wear on shoes. Already in the 1860s mechanization was coming to the shoemaking business and by 1909, when this photograph was taken, village craftsmen would buy most of the cheaper items from the factories of Northampton and Leicester. The ready availability of cheap shoes from multiple retailers in the market towns soon reduced the surviving village cobblers to doing little more than repair work.

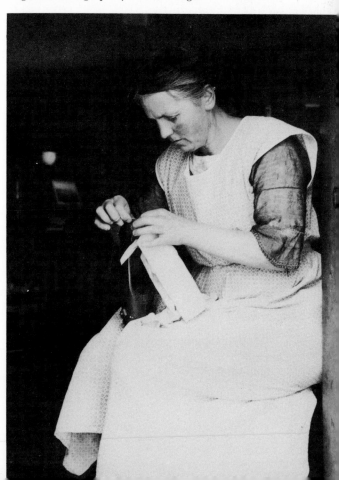

41 *Below* Glove-making in Worcestershire, 1920. This was one of the more important of domestic employments for village women. Gloves were cut out in factories, mostly in the towns, and were taken to domestic workers to be stitched up. This was a trade based mainly in western counties, from Devon to Worcestershire, although Oxfordshire was the centre, with the largest factories at Woodstock and Charlbury. There was also work on a smaller scale for village workers throughout most of England. Photograph by Miss M. Wight.

40 *Above* Making oak baskets, Worcestershire, 1935. By the end of the thirties the number of basketmakers was falling, especially in the countryside. The availability of cheap imported baskets was one of the main reasons for this. Photograph by Miss M. Wight.

42 *Above* During the 1890s one result of concern about the movement of population away from the villages was the introduction of technical training, in the hope that this would enable people to remain in rural employment. Berkshire County Council, as shown here, provided a travelling school in farriery to improve the knowledge and skills of blacksmiths. Instruction was given both in smithing and on the anatomy of the horse's foot from a van equipped with fires, anvils, vices and other equipment. The photograph dates from 1898.

43 *Opposite, above* Thatching was one of the ancient rural crafts which, though declining, survived throughout this period. In the mid-nineteenth century thatchers were still in great demand for roofing ricks of corn. A decline in the acreage of corn reduced the amount of work, although it was not until after 1945 that combine harvesters and plastic sheeting completely killed off this side of the business. Domestic work remained, and even began to increase slightly as townsmen recently moved to the country began to smarten up old cottages, or, as this photograph of 1939 shows, brewers refurbished their public houses. Most likely taken in Wiltshire by Miss M. Wight.

44 Corn-milling, formerly a thriving part of village life, was undermined from the 1870s onwards by the building of large flour mills at the major ports, which used mainly imported wheat. By the 1890s country windmills and watermills were being closed. Ockford Mill in Surrey was kept busy, as this early-twentieth-century postcard shows. However, the load on the wagon and the signs on the wall reveal that business was not in flour-milling, but in hay and grains for animal feeding-stuffs.

45 In districts with a good supply of clay, brickmaking often numbered among village occupations. Eventually, mass-produced bricks from yards at Peterborough or Bedford destroyed the local trade. But there were plenty of village brickmakers still busy around 1900 when this photograph was taken.

46 The foundry at Smyth and Son's agricultural implement works, Peasenhall, Suffolk. Smyth's had been established at the beginning of the nineteenth century, and became one of the foremost manufacturers of seed drills in the country. In expanding so, the firm brought factory-based work to this village.

Two ancillary activities of farming which farmers began to take more seriously as prices of cereals fell:

47 Cleaning eggs on a farm at Hoole, Cheshire, 1936.

48 Making sausages, Essex, 1936.

Shops and Markets

49 The Bell Inn at Woodham Walter, in Essex, with a somewhat profuse growth of ivy. On the left is perhaps a farmer out in his carriage and, on the right, attached to the cart, is a mowing machine.

50 Sheep being driven to market through the streets of Corfe, Dorset. The dog has evidently marshalled his flock with the camera in mind.

51 The post office and general store at Ecchinswell, near Newbury, in 1913. It was housed in what was then quite a modern building providing ample living accommodation for Mr Trigg's family. The importance of the bicycle for local transport in the country is clearly shown, with various machines possessed by customers and the postman outside the shop. And in the sheds at the side, Mr Trigg has a shop for the sale and repair of bicycles.

52 Mr Varndell, with his son Ernest, about to set out on his baker's round in Twyford, Berkshire *c.* 1895. His shop is one of the modern terraces, complete with gas lighting, in this village which was growing through the influence of nearby Reading, and of London.

53 *Opposite above* A shop at Cheddar catering for the tourist trade, including, to judge from one sign, Australian visitors! As well as the cream teas and local cheese, there is a little display of postcards on the door.

55 *Above* A butcher's shop in the village of Haddenham, Buckinghamshire, with what one supposes is a fresh consignment of meat arriving outside. The muddiness of roads before motor traffic can be seen from this winter's view of around 1910.

54 The bold selling methods of the end of the nineteenth century come to Midsomer Norton, Somerset. Welch & Co. seem to have been general dealers, advertising themselves as grocers, drapers and ladies' outfitters, but the style of their shop is very different from the small village store of photograph 20. The fairly long exposures needed for photography, even on a bright day, are evident from the ghostly figures of passers-by.

56 During the interwar years village retailing began to cater more for the passing tourist. Seen here is a stall of rustic charm selling fresh fruit and farm produce to visitors to Weston sub Edge, Gloucestershire in 1939. Photograph by Miss M. Wight.

57 Milk being loaded for delivery at an Essex farm in 1931. Many farmers who went into dairying decided to take on direct retailing of their milk, especially if they farmed reasonably close to a town.

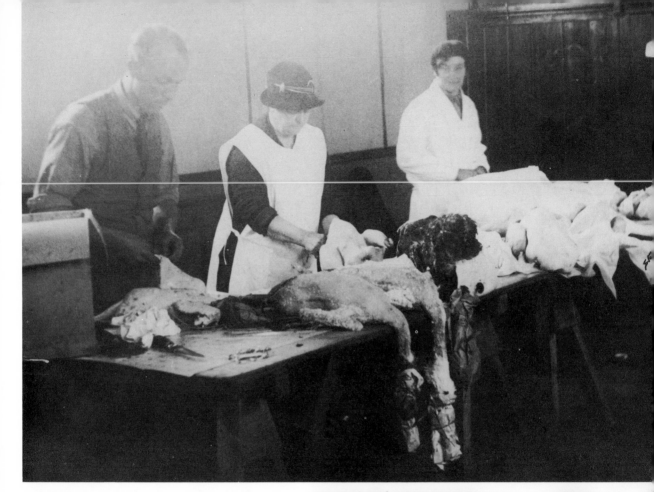

58 Women's Institutes brought a new element into rural trading, with their markets for home-made produce. Two members and presumably a co-opted helper, of the Ringwood and Shelfleet branch, are dressing turkeys for the Christmas market on the Isle of Wight in 1935.

59 One of the newer forms of village trade at the end of this period: a toffee apple shop in the West Country, 1936. A Miss M. Wight photograph.

Domestic Life

60 Perhaps this picture fits in with the popular imagination of the old country cottage—neat thatch, a large and rambling garden, and of course sunshine. But the idyll is diminished a little by the realization of just how small is the cottage, and by the obvious fact that life is hard work in a home with no mains services.

61 *Above* A cottage parlour in Somerset with an open fire used for cooking. According to *Country Life*, which published the photograph in 1911, the old woman sitting in the inglenook had been born in this house, had never left the village and had never seen either a train or a bus. Victorian industrial culture had reached her to some extent, though; most of the mugs and plates arranged above the fireplace are of Staffordshire ware.

62 *Opposite above* Making butter on a farm near Blanchland, Northumberland. The dairymaids are rolling out freshly churned butter on a butterworker to squeeze out excess moisture. On the left is a barrel churn.

63 *Right* A bread oven of the type built into the kitchen wall of farmhouses and some cottages. The box at the front is full of faggots ready for use in heating the oven. Once the correct temperature was reached, the ashes were swept out and bread put in. Of course, not all cottagers possessed such an oven. Those who did not, if they baked their own bread, had to use a neighbour's or the baker's oven. The photograph is from Thorpe-by-Water, Rutland, taken in 1913.

64 *Above left* The kitchenmaid, preparing a meal in a farmhouse, probably in the 1890s.

66 *Above* Where piped water was laid on, it was usually the occasion for some celebration. This photograph shows the crowds assembled at Stratton, Cornwall, for the opening in 1903 of the new water supply from the Tamar Lake reservoir on the old Bude canal.

65 *Left* Collecting water at Avebury, Wiltshire, in the 1930s. Even in 1939 only the largest villages were likely to be connected to mains water supply and drainage. The reasons were simple. There was no pressing urgency on public-health grounds to arrange mains services, as there had been in the large towns. Moreover, the capital cost of laying the pipes was usually too high for the Rural District Councils to manage. A Miss M. Wight photograph.

Electricity supply was extended into rural areas during the interwar years. It offered villagers new domestic comforts. Its disadvantages are perhaps shown in these photographs taken by the Council for the Preservation of Rural England, designed to show disfigurement of the countryside by modern developments.

67 The village of Giggleswick in the Pennines of north Yorkshire, June 1933, showing several modern additions to its landscape: telegraph poles; public telephone; litter around the benches, an influence perhaps of tourism.

68 An advertising hoarding by the small substation at Totley, Derbyshire, a village by now becoming a suburb of Sheffield, as the type of houses in the background indicate.

Schools and Schoolchildren

69 Dame school at Vale cottage, Castle End Road, Ruscombe, Berkshire, c. 1860. The school was run by Mary Ann Wadhams together with her sister-in-law, Jane Wadhams and cousin, Sarah Lunn, from approximately 1856 to 1876. Mary's husband ran the local bakery, but was also a plumber, glazier and house-painter.

70 *Right* Weybourne village school, Surrey (erected by John Knight), became a Sunday school after a larger public elementary school was built at Hale in 1895. Note the school bell on the roof and blocked entrance into the playground.

71 *Below* Radstock Church of England school, Somerset, June 1912. The school was built in 1850 and enlarged in 1884, 1893 and 1898. It was controlled by six managers and had about 400 pupils (boys, girls and infants) at the time this photograph was taken. The boys shown here are in the second form of the upper school, and are all wearing a buttonhole for the occasion.

72 *Below right* Sunday school, at the Assembly Rooms, Twyford, Berkshire, 1912. The photograph shows the intermediate catechism held for 8–10 year olds; the little catechism was for those up to eight. The church year book (1910–13) for St Mary's, Twyford, reveals that there was a Catechism Provident (a slate club) into which payments of 1d. to 4d. could be made. There was a bonus for 40 attendances at the catechisms.

73 *Opposite above* Sunday school outing, using Patchett's wagon from Mapleton farm, Horsington, Lincs, *c.* 1908. The wagon is a Lincolnshire box-type, decked out with floral garlands; the horses are wearing full harness and head decorations, and have been well groomed for the occasion.

74 Empire day at the Chase, Farnham Royal, Buckinghamshire, 1905. The children are clearly being addressed on a patriotic theme, but for some the camera holds more fascination. The two boys in the immediate foreground seem fully absorbed in their own conversation. A Wilder photograph.

75 *Above* The school house of a Somerset school, decorated to celebrate the Coronation of Edward VII.

76 As part of their education, country children were often taken to see village craftsmen and other rural tradesmen at work; the expectation was that most would seek local employment after leaving school. The photograph shows the top sawyer directing the cut while the bottom sawyer helps pull the pitsaw through the wood. The pitman would get covered in dust and generally received a free allocation of beer in addition to his wages. Taken in Herefordshire by Miss M. Wight in the late 1920s.

77 School milk. The Government sought to improve child nutrition from the mid-1930s by providing free milk to needy schoolchildren, while subsidizing it to others. One quart of milk was held to be equal to 4 oz of bacon or 1 lb of lean meat. The photograph shows children at Cranbourne school, Potters Bar, Middlesex on 28 December 1938. Schools were sometimes kept open during the holidays for the distribution of milk—in this case the classrooms were especially heated for the 250 children who turned up.

Public Services

78 Devon constabulary, *c.* 1889. This Wilder photograph shows an off-duty village policeman with his wife and two children. By this time the village bobby had become a familiar and comforting sight, and professional policing played a large part in reducing the level of violent crime which had characterized the English countryside in the first half of the nineteenth century. As Edwin Grey noted of his Hertfordshire childhood:

'I should say that the village and indeed the whole of the parish was, in the days of my boyhood and youth, free from any serious crime, for I can remember nothing more startling than an occasional affray, or fowl-stealing case, a public house fight, a neighbour's squabble or maybe a few cases of petty theft, principally of fruit from some nearby orchard.' (*Cottage Life in a Hertfordshire Village*, Fisher Knight 1934).

79 Somerset constabulary, undated. From 1856 it was obligatory on all counties to establish a paid police force, the intention being to create a highly disciplined and efficient body of men. Lord Normanby's rules required that a candidate had 'to be able to read and write, was intelligent and active and certified to be free from bodily complaint and of a strong constitution; and be recommended as of irreproachable character and connections'. Despite the long hours and gruelling nature of the work—all patrolling was on foot and up to twenty miles might be covered in a day—the police force was an attractive occupation to young countrymen. It offered responsibility, security and the opportunity of self-advancement.

80 *Opposite* The recorder of Devizes, 1911. At this time the recorder would have been an experienced barrister appointed to conduct borough quarter sessions, and was responsible for trying medium-to-serious (but not the most serious) crimes, committed in an incorporated borough. Villagers who committed such offences in their own locality would come instead before a county court; murder cases would be tried by a crown court, while petty crime would be dealt with by local justices sitting in petty sessions. A Wilder photograph.

81 Special constable on duty in Herefordshire in 1935, when Queen Mary was due to drive past. Photograph by Miss M. Wight.

82 The reform of local government and the setting up of county and rural district councils in 1888 and 1894 brought new services to the village. Here council officials are trying to prevent waste of water, near Tewkesbury in Gloucestershire in September 1934. The workman is listening with a large stethoscope for sounds of water leakage on the mains.

83 Manual fire engine, Somerset, *c.* 1910. The firemen look as though they practised their drill regularly; their stance suggests a team about to race with a gun-carriage at a military tournament.

84 Twyford and Ruscombe fire brigade, Berkshire. The brigade was formed in 1875, as a result of a fire that devastated Mud Row, when, it was said, a boy was sent on a bicycle to call the Reading brigade. In Reading, an argument as to whether to send the County or the Borough engine—both horse-drawn—caused further delay and the destruction of a shop and seven cottages. Twyford's manual engine was disposed of a year later and a horse-drawn, steam fire engine, known as 'Stroller', acquired in 1877. The photograph shows Stroller and the brigade in front of the fire station. On the left is Henry Maynard, the Captain between 1901 and 1916. At this time the firemen were called by whistle—although electric call bells were hoped for—and a local horse-owner used to lend the brigade a pair of horses at two guineas a fire. It is not known when Stroller went out of service or what replaced it.

85 Old friends' almshouse, Bridport, Dorset, 1890. Before the introduction of old-age pensions in 1908, the more fortunate among the aged poor were able to spend their last years in an almshouse, maintained by a local charity. Here they could live with some degree of comfort and dignity, and, best of all, avoid the horror of being sent to a workhouse.

SPEEDY AND HONOURABLE RETURN
TO THE ABSENT-MINDED BEGGAR

SUCCESS TO LORD ROBERTS AND
HER MAJESTY'S FORCES IN SOUTH AFRICA

86 Wokingham workhouse, January 1900. The things most resented about the workhouse were the stigma of pauperism, the separation of married couples and the general harshness of the regime. Towards the end of the nineteenth century conditions improved, but even when workhouses offered a reasonable diet, warmth and kindness, the feeling that admittance was somehow a disgrace persisted. In this photograph the new century is being celebrated, and with it the hope that Kipling's 'absent-minded beggar' will return victorious from the South African war.

87 Cold Ash Cottage Hospital for children, Berkshire *c.* 1907. The cottage hospital movement dates from the 1860s; hospitals were at first set up in converted cottages and catered for six to ten patients at a time. Medical treatment was provided by a resident nurse and by regular visits from a local GP. Although the cottage hospital was a step forward in providing care for the rural sick, the fact that patients were charged acted as a deterrent, and poorer families continued to nurse most illnesses at home for many years to come.

Church and Chapel

88 The quarterly meeting of the Bude circuit of the Methodist Church; the group gathered at Underhill, Welcome, Devon on 24 June 1909. The photograph illustrates changes in society reaching the churches, for this was the first occasion when women were allowed to attend these meetings.

89 The Bishop of Oxford arriving at Sibford Ferris, Oxfordshire, for the dedication of a new piece of graveyard, 8 May 1902.

90 The bellringers of Willersey, near Broadway in Worcestershire, displaying a remarkable profusion of headgear.

91 Queen Victoria's Diamond Jubilee was the occasion for memorials in villages up and down the country. At Farnham Royal, Buckinghamshire, new bells were cast for the church and are seen here being prepared for hanging in 1898. A Wilder photograph.

92 A vicarage tea party, at Chilcompton, Somerset, at the turn of the century. This feast was evidently given for the children of the village, who, faced with the camera, seem uncertain whether to smile, keep eating, or scowl. The last option seems to have won.

Traditional Customs

93 Morris dancers at Bucknell, Oxfordshire, *c.* 1875. This is believed to be the earliest known picture of the Morris. The custom had its origins in prehistoric rites, by which our ancestors sought to influence nature and the fertility of crops. It had all but died out as a living tradition by the late nineteenth century, although often lovingly revived by churchmen, schoolteachers and other antiquarians.

94 *Above left* Hooden horse, St Nicholas at Wade, Kent, *c.* 1908. Strange animal figures are associated with many mid-winter folk rituals. Here the man-horse, accompanied by other characters, paraded around the village at Christmas, knocking at each house. When the door was opened, the horse kicked, reared, neighed and acted in as frightening a manner as possible. At the same time a man dressed as an old woman (seen on the left of the photograph) swept the feet of the door-opener with a besom. If the company was allowed to enter a red ribbon was tied to the horse's head, and carol-singing and other merry-making followed. The visit conferred luck on the house, and in return the visitors were offered ale, cakes and other refreshments.

95 *Left* Horn dance, Abbots Bromley, late 1920s. Performed on the Monday after 4 September, this ceremony commemorates the restoration of lost forest rights during the reign of Henry III, but the character of the dance is much older. It appears to be the acting out of a hunt, the purpose of which is to bring success to the hunters by imitative magic. The six leading dancers represent deer, and carry reindeer skulls pressed against their chests, so that their heads and shoulders are masked by the antlers. They dance to an accordion and triangle. With them are two musicians, a man dressed as Robin Hood, another representing Maid Marion, a Fool in cap and bells, and a man with crossbow and arrows. Robin Hood is mounted on a hobby-horse, whose jaws are snapped in time with the music. After the first dance is over, the deer-men proceed through the parish, visiting farmhouses and cottages, bringing good fortune to the inhabitants. Photograph by George Long.

96 *Above* Mummers, Overton, Hampshire, late 1920s. The mummers seen here are performing Johnny Jack's play. Although mainly of the 'hero-combat' type, it is confused by the number of antagonists; one unnamed 'Son of Father Christmas', Bold Slasher, the Turkish Knight and Twing-Twang (alias Johnny Jack). Part of the dialogue is sung, and the play concludes with the salutation 'God bless the mistress of this house'. Performance took place between Christmas and New Year, when all principal residents of Overton and neighbouring villages were visited. According to the local postmistress, the play became extinct at the beginning of the Second World War when the old people who had preserved it were sent from their cottages to the workhouse, to make room for workers at the paper-mill at Laverstock. Photograph by George Long.

97 Biddenden dole, Kent, late 1920s. Local folklore
reports that this charity was founded in the twelfth
century by twin sisters, Eliza and Mary Chulkhurst, who
left 20 acres of land, still called the Bread and Cheese
lands, to provide an annual dole of bread, cheese and beer
at Easter for the poor of the parish. Whether there is any
truth in this is doubtful, but parish records show that the
dole has been distributed for at least 300 years. The
distribution of beer is not mentioned after the mid-
seventeenth century, but bread and cheese and a
Biddenden cake are still given annually to each claimant
in need on Easter Monday while cakes are also
distributed to visitors who come to watch the proceedings.
Photograph by George Long.

Recreation and Leisure

98 Inside the Crooked Billet public house, Stoke Row, Oxfordshire, in the 1920s. Although this is a posed photograph, by P. O. Collier of Reading, there can be no doubt that the labourer on the right is occupying a favourite seat. Interestingly, he is holding a Mocha ware beer mug. This inexpensive type of earthenware originated early in the nineteenth century, and was so named because of its resemblance to the quartz known as mocha-stone. The body of the mug is white, banded with blue, over which a brown pigment has been spread into markings suggesting trees or moss. Such mugs were commonly found in nineteenth century pubs bearing the excise mark of the weights and measure office; their survival is rare.

99 *Opposite above* White Horse hotel, Downton, Wiltshire, late 1930s. The darts match is being played by members of the Downton Pig Club, and photographed by *Farmer and Stockbreeder* for an article on successful village pig clubs. The proprietor of the pub was Geo. N. Jones, who also owned the local butcher's shop. The card to the right of the dart-board bears the rhyme:

'A man who drinks strong beer
and goes to bed right mellow
Lives as he ought to live
And dies a Jolly Good Fellow'

101 *Above* Welton Jazz Band, Somerset, 1919. The occasion is unknown, although the ex-soldier in the second row bears the legend 'Victory 1919' on his cap, suggesting that the hamlet may be celebrating the return from the war of some, at least, of its young men.

100 *Left* Yattendon minstrels, Berkshire, 1896. Traditional folk-songs were replaced in popularity towards the end of the nineteenth century by new forms of music, including minstrel songs. The photograph shows one such minstrel band, rigged out in very colourful costumes with carefully blacked faces, performing at Yattendon Court, the home of Alfred Waterhouse Esq., RA.

102 *Above* Punch and Judy show, part of the Queen Victoria Jubilee festivities, held at Herringstone House, near Winterbourne Herringstone, Dorset, 1887.

103 *Opposite above* Tea party for village children at Sulham Rectory, Berkshire late 1890s. The camera has not captured the details of the meal, other than the enormous plate of cherries set in the middle of the table. The wild flowers have surely been picked by the children themselves and set down, in homely fashion, in a jam jar. A Wilder photograph.

104 Gipsy children dancing at a New Forest fair, 1909. Photograph by E. M. Howard of Lyndhurst, Hampshire.

New Forest 'Gips'

105 'Kissing cousins' at a fete, Yateley, Hampshire, late 1920s. A naval touch to the occasion is provided by the officer in dress uniform standing in the background, as well as by the little boy in his naval suit. His young female companion seems unimpressed by his attentions. Photograph by Eric Guy.

106 'Playing for the pig', skittles at Sibford Ferris fete, 1916. The fete was held at Holmley House, in aid of the Red Cross, and this game brought in about £4.0-0. A number of wounded soldiers may be seen on the left of the photograph.

107 Donkey ride at Burnham Beeches, Bucks, *c.* 1892.
Nothing more is known about the events taking place. A
Wilder photograph.

108 Alresford fair, Hampshire, probably late 1920s. This was famous as a sheep fair, held on the second Thursday in July, but there were other pleasureable attractions too. The children are clearly enjoying the ride, even though the roundabout is a fairly crude piece of machinery, worked by manpower alone. It must have required considerable strength to get started, although once in motion, would have been relatively easy to keep going. Photograph by Eric Guy.

109 The Vaudeville Electric Theatre, 47–8 Broad Street, Reading, 1909. By this time increased personal mobility brought village people regularly into the towns for entertainment. The electric theatre, showing moving pictures, was all the rage; the cheapness of the seats bringing the 'world's latest productions' (as advertised here) to a mass audience. Cinema owners often commissioned 'newsreel' films of local interest, which

were very popular with patrons. A film showing the christening of a local training ship has been retained 'by special request'. Photograph by P. O. Collier.

111 Ordinary country people also enjoyed an excursion to the seaside; as here in the 'Starling' motor bus outing to Little Wakering, Southend, September 1926. Perhaps this was a special occasion of some sort, as many younger men and women would have been employed on the harvest at this time of year. Observe how the Castle Inn is catering for the growing tourist trade, offering teas and refreshments, fruit and flowers, Lukers fine sparkling ales, and wines and spirits. Despite a hot and sunny day, all of the trippers remain resolutely clad in their Sunday-best suits and coats.

110 Clovelly High Street, Devon, *c.* 1900. The visitors to this quaint seaside village are mainly middle-class, and have probably come a short journey by trap or motor-car. A few may be genuine holiday-makers, but everyone has been careful to wear a hat or hoist an umbrella to protect themselves from the sun. Photograph by William Pinder Thompson.

112 & 113 For many village children, there was a host of
more simple enjoyments, as in climbing on a wagon (note
the girl's tattered plimsolls) or in taking a bathe in the
local river. Both photographs were taken in the late 1930s
by Miss M. Wight.

Games and Sport

114 Girl with hoop, at Tidmarsh, Berkshire *c.* 1894. A Wilder photograph.

115 *Opposite above* Village children at play, Sulham, Berkshire 1890s. The boy has obviously been placed in the stocks for the benefit of the camera, while his companion—also with a hoop—looks less pleased at having his game interrupted. The girls are all dressed in adult style, although their sturdy and muddied boots say much about the state of village roads at this time. A Wilder photograph.

117 *Above* Tennis tournament, staged by Purley Lawn Tennis club, Berkshire, 1895. The game became a national craze after the introduction of the Wimbledon championships in 1877. The photograph shows a number of doubles matches in progress; apparently in such 'genteel' company umpiring was considered unnecessary. Already, tennis 'whites' seem to be almost obligatory for both men and women. A Wilder photograph.

116 Children being taught croquet, Sulham, Berkshire, 1900. Croquet had been replaced by tennis as a competitive sport, although the distinctive click of mallet against ball was still a familiar sound on country-house lawns around the turn of the century. It is interesting to note that the children are wearing smock-like garments as a cover-all, an example of the adoption of a rustic style by more fashionable people. A Wilder photograph.

CHILTON LODGE CRICKET TEAM, LADIES. V. GENTS 1913

118 *Opposite* Mixed cricket match, Berkshire 1913. The men do not appear to be taking the ladies' challenge too seriously, although the result of this good-humoured encounter is not recorded.

120 *Above* Village athletic match, *c.* 1910. As the older forms of rural sport—such as animal baiting and prize fighting—were suppressed in the second half of the nineteenth century, they were replaced by more disciplined and organized events, often under the patronage of the local landowners or parson. Here, at the start of the 100 yards, each lane has been carefully marked by lengths of cord, ensuring a fair opportunity to each contestant.

119 Hurst football club, winners of the Wargrave and district league, Berkshire, 1908–9.

121 Pigeon fancying, Somerset. While many of the new sports were highly organized spectator events, some working men preferred more solitary though no less competitive pursuits. Pigeon fancying developed initially in industrial villages and towns, requiring little space and little expenditure, except on the birds themselves. Not everyone, however, welcomed the new hobby; as early as 1823 R. Guest deplored the decline of the old 'manly' and 'vigorous exercises', noting that 'the present pursuits and pleasures of the labouring classes are of a more effeminate cast . . . they are now Pigeon-fanciers, Canary-breeders, and Tulip growers'.

122 The gentry and farmers, however, remained faithful to such traditional pastimes as shooting. In D. P. Blaine's opinion, expressed without conscious irony in 1890, the sport 'constituted the healthful and rational recreation of thousands'. The photograph shows a shooting party at Bradley, Hampshire, 1887.

123 Villagers often indulged a different talent: that of outwitting the gamekeeper, both to supplement their diet and for the sheer excitement of doing so. Seen here is a Dorset gamekeeper with an old cottager, probably 1880s. Note the straw-thatched bee skeps outside the cottage doorway.

124 'Landing over a stiff Devon bank', *Country Life*, 30 November 1907. Women began to hunt in the 1850s when the social exclusivity of the sport was still firmly established, although decorum dictated that they rode side-saddle in all-embracing riding habits. This rider is obviously an accomplished practitioner of this difficult art.

125 Meet at Broadway, Gloucestershire, probably in the late 1920s or early 1930s. With the growth of subscription packs in the second half of the nineteenth century, the hunt was open to a wider membership. Even those who could not participate directly could enjoy the thrills of spectatorship—or follow as best they could by car or on bicycle. Note the 'nippy' crossing the road with the 'stirrup cups' for the riders.

Communications

126 Already by 1860 the inland waterways were declining as a means of transport for rural produce, as the trade was captured by the railways. Even the traffic remaining hardly obtruded on the village as most passed by on its way from town to town. By the 1930s peaceful scenes such as this were the most common. It is probably on the Kennet and Avon canal, this being within the main working area of the photographer, Eric Guy.

Three types of transport on and around the farm:

129 *Above* The motor lorry began to make a significant impression on the rural scene after the First World War.

127 *Opposite above* Horses were the main source of motive power on the farm throughout the period covered by this book. Two horses in line stand with a dung cart outside a fairly impressive barn on a farm in Herefordshire in the 1930s.

128 Early tractors were often used for general haulage work. Indeed, early machines were perhaps more successful in road haulage than field work, where mud and rough surfaces often proved too much for them. The tractor shown here, presumably taking a wagon load of corn to market, seems to be on a trial run, to judge from the close attention it is receiving.

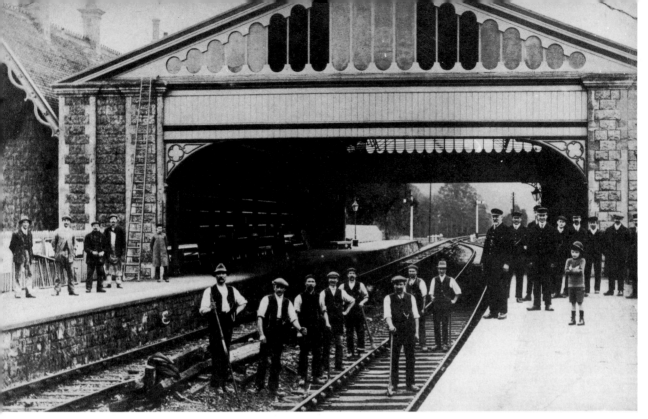

130 Cheddar railway station, Somerset, with work in progress on the tracks and on the roof. The station staff are on the right, a fairly large body of men, although Cheddar was one of the bigger village stations.

131 This photograph was probably taken in the late 1870s and shows something of the end of an era in country transport. During the seventeenth and eighteenth centuries, roads throughout the country had been placed in the hands of turnpike trusts who charged tolls to pay for the upkeep of the roads. The railways caused traffic to fall so much that the trusts became uneconomic and they were abolished—less than 200 remained by 1881. The photograph shows another change that came over village life at this time, for just one man is wearing a smock; the rest are in ordinary jackets. We have no information as to where this toll gate was.

132 Road mending could be a valuable source of casual employment for the labourers of the village. Here a group of roadmen is at work in Somerset before the First World War. Motor transport had not yet made its impact here, for the road surface is still mainly compacted stone chips with a generous layer of mud.

133 Public transport in the villages during the nineteenth century was in the hands of the carriers, who provided regular services into the towns mainly on market days. Some dense networks of these services grew up. As well as this van from Burghfield more than 90 carriers came into Reading in the 1890s. It was not a form of transport for anyone in a hurry. Progress was leisurely, on a circuitous route with many stops to pick up and deliver parcels.

134 *Opposite above* An engineers' gang from the GPO telegraphs department having a break from their work in 1908. The telegraph system had been started in the 1830s, the telephones in the 1870s. Both were to have a great impact on village life, bringing it closer to that of the towns. The effects were felt more slowly in the country than in the towns: only a few of the wealthier people and more substantial businesses of the village had a telephone in the 1930s.

136 *Above* The village postman of 1939, this time provided with a motorcycle and sidecar, outside the Post Office at Rampisham in Dorset. Photograph by Miss M. Wight.

135 The staff of the post office at Cheddar, Somerset, a busy office serving a large village and the demands of tourism. A photograph from around 1900.

The effects of motor transport on the countryside:

137 The new trade of garage-proprietor was introduced to the village. At Merrow, Surrey, in common with many other villages, the blacksmith opened a garage alongside his forge. It will be seen that the entrance to the workshop is horseshoe-shaped. The photograph is from 1927.

138 The first motor-bus services in rural areas were established in the first years of this century, and were often operated by railway companies as feeder services in the more remote parts of the country. After the first World War numerous new firms entered the motor-bus business, such as Nogus Brothers who worked from the small village of Herongate, between Brentwood and Tilbury, in Essex. This is the scene outside the Boar's Head, Herongate, used as the bus terminus in 1928.

Village Visitors

The tedium of village life was relieved by a steady stream of visitors: itinerant tradesmen, entertainers, politicians and missionaries, medical quacks and the health-conscious denizens of the industrial cities—who increasingly sought fresh air and green fields to renew their vitality.

139 G. Dixie Parker, of Launceston, Cornwall, *c.* 1900. Knife grinders and cutlers, who could turn their hand to a host of small repair jobs, such as fixing the spokes of this umbrella, continued to tour the villages and eke out a modest living into the interwar period.

JAMES MOORE
THE LOCAL PEDLAR

141 *Below* Gipsies selling daffodils at Malvern Link, Worcestershire, 1939. Some gipsy families might wander the lengths of the country, while others, like the Smiths shown here, might keep to a locality so that it was possible to become acquainted with their rounds and know where to find them almost to the week. Ernest Pulbrook, writing in the 1920s, noted that 'few speak well of the gipsy and his like' because 'no doubt they poach and do not put themselves out to find the owner of a wandering dog or straying hen, light a fire beneath a notice board forbidding them to do so, and occasionally keep the police courts busy over a fractious fight', but 'experience has proved that they are more courteous to strangers than others with more advantages'. Photograph by Miss M. Wight.

140 *Above* James Moore, of Wadebridge, Cornwall. The pedlar sold ribbons, threads, packets of pins, and small novelties to poor families, who could just afford the few pennies they cost. As rural incomes gradually rose and shops spread into rural areas, the itinerant trade declined. Pedlars were a comparatively rare sight by the time this postcard was published, by J. E. Oatley of Wadebridge, in *c.* 1920.

142 Organ grinder, Sulham, Berkshire, 1894. One of the
numerous band of travelling entertainers on the road in
the late nineteenth century; others included the ballad
singer, acrobat, one-man band, and the animal trainer
with his performing bear or small menagerie. The
building shown in the photograph is Rectory Lodge and
the children are most likely from the village school,
rebuilt by the Rector, Rev. John Wilder, in 1892 at his
expense, for about 50 pupils. The average attendance in
1895 was 35 and the school mistress was Miss Amy Grist.
A Wilder photograph.

143 Meeting of the Red Van of the English Land
Restoration League, Grandborough, Warwickshire,
1894. The Red Vanners advocated giving the land 'back
to the people' from whom it had been taken at the time of
the enclosures. Their long treks through the English
counties during the years 1892–7 were bitterly resented
by the property-owning classes and the Tory press. The
Cambridge Chronicle on 6 May 1892 noted that a van 'has
been perambulating the villages of East Anglia, and
socialism and sedition have been spread broadcast'. The
League enjoyed early success in Suffolk where a labourer
commented 'wherever that red cart of yours has been the
men have got a bob or two extra', but by 1896 Fred
Verinder, one of the organizers, found 'almost everywhere
the farmer—at once the victim and tool of the landlord—
is master of the situation'.

144 The inventor of the 'Ivel' cross-frame racing safety
bicycle, an early world record-beater, in 1886. Cycling
began as a recreation for the better-off, but technical
improvements and mass-production meant that reliable
machines could be purchased by urban working people
by the 1890s. The popularity of the sport was spread by
the élitist Cyclists' Touring Club as well as by labour
organizations, such as the Clarion Club, which aimed at
combining healthy exercise with preaching socialism in
the countryside. The photograph shows Dan Albone, a
mechanical genius, who manufactured cycles and motor-
cycles at Biggleswade in Bedfordshire, and went on to
make the first successful agricultural tractor produced in
England. His premature death in 1906 was a major blow
for Britain's early motor industry.

145 'An afternoon's spin': cyclists outside the Bladebone Inn, Bucklebury, Berkshire, *c. 1900*. Notice the man is holding a map to enable him and his partner to penetrate deeply into 'unknown territory'; his bicycle is parked against the paling in the background. A Wilder photograph.

The growth of the 'open-air' movement in the interwar period brought many more visitors into the countryside: tourism was to provide rural people with new opportunities to make a living and to complain about the way in which their privacy and solitude was being invaded.

146 Walking in the Lake District in the late 1920s.

147 'Getting away from it all on a motor-bike', from the *Open Air* magazine, 1924.

Village Clubs and Societies

148 Members of the Henton Friendly Society, Somerset, marching through the village, to the sound of the local brass band. They are wearing sashes fixed with rosettes and carrying the brass poleheads which were the emblem of their particular society. Most villages at this time supported one or several such mutual benefit associations. Members paid a few pence each week into a common fund, from which they were entitled to draw in sickness or old age, and which insured a decent burial. Focusing on the local pub, with the landlord as treasurer, the society also organized a feast day each year—an important part of which was the club walk through the village. The photograph was taken in May 1910.

149 Scene from 'Conjurer Lintern', with the original cast of Camel Play Actors. The aim of this band of rural players, coming from the villages of Queen and West Camel in Somerset, was to perform plays written in their own dialect and dealing with local traditions, stories and everyday life. In the front row are Mr Burgess, Farmer Hoare, Dr John Read and Farmer Brain. Taken in April 1912.

John Read recalled in his book, *Farmers Joy* (1958), that 'The dramatic season at Camel was determined by the exigencies of cider-making on the one hand and of potato planting on the other. One needed little acquaintance with Camel folk in order to realize that "a man 'ud be a born zatty to lef a cheese up in wring-house, half-ground down, vur to go up-street to gape at a play". So also when "the days did begin to draw out" a man was bound in duty to his family "to spuddly round a bit in the dimpsies, to get his gearn all hand-pat and vitty vur drapping in the cheddies come Good Vriday"; naturally a man was not going to risk his potato crop by venturing to "zet" it on any other day. That is why the Camel Play-Actors used to cluster round the fire "up in the schoolroom" on cold, frosty nights between November and March.'

Billiard Room, Village Hall, Nettlebed.

150 Nettlebed village hall, Oxfordshire, *c.* 1921. Village halls provided a centre for community life, and the interwar period saw a middle-class 'movement' to create more of them, especially to offset the growing attraction of urban entertainments. Photograph by P. O. Collier.

152 Young Farmers' Club, Kingsclere, Berkshire. The photograph shows the show and sale at Mr Breen's farm, 1922. Sir William Price, the YFC President, is congratulating Gerald Webb, aged nine, after presenting him with a first prize in one of the events. The first club was founded in Devon in 1921, as the result of an initiative by United Dairies. Despite the early support of Lord Northcliffe and the *Daily Mail*, the number of clubs grew only slowly until 1936 when County Council grant aid facilitated the formation of county federations. By 1939 there were 412 clubs, with about 15,000 members, organized in some 20 county federations under national leadership.

151 Wootton Bridge Women's Institute, Isle of Wight, June 1933. The Women's Institute was founded in 1915, although at that time few saw any need for women's organizations besides the Mothers' Union and church and chapel groups. But the WI soon expanded into a wide range of activities—art classes, choral singing, helping in local hospitals, and running market stalls. By 1939 most villages possessed their own branch.

153 Paulton Troop Scouts, Somerset, 1918. The influence of the war can be seen in the Scoutmaster's army uniform, as well as in the determined expressions on the faces of many of the boys. Their staves are held rigidly to attention.

154 Girl Guide Troop, late 1920s. Sadly neither the name of the company nor the place have been recorded. The guides, like the scouts, were intended to foster not only patriotism in young people, but also a sense of local pride and service to the community. This group has been enrolled by a branch of the Council for the Preservation of Rural England, to clear up litter after the departure of urban trippers.

Politics

155 Electioneering at East Tisted, Hampshire. William Wickham, the candidate supported here, was returned as Conservative member for East Hampshire (Petersfield division) in the general election of 1892. He defeated the Gladstonian Liberal, J. Bonham Carter, by 3,912 votes to 3,008. In the 1895 election he was returned unopposed, but died two years later. The Reform Act of 1884 extended the suffrage to all male householders, thus giving the agricultural labourer and rural worker the vote.

156 *Opposite above* Electioneering at Wells, Somerset. The Hon. G. Hylton Jolliffe, addressing the crowd from the balcony, was returned as Conservative member for the Wells division in the general election of 1895, beating the Gladstonian Liberal, B. Morice, by 4,696 votes to 3,286. Shortly after this Jolliffe became Lord Hylton and did not contest the next election.

158 *Above* Meeting of the Eastern Counties Agricultural Labourers' and Smallholders' Union, addressed by its General Secretary, George Edwards (standing in wagon; also present Tom Higdon, second from left, and Herbert Day, second from right). This may have been taken during the long strike of the St Faith's branch of the union, which lasted from May 1910 to January 1911. The labourers asked for a shilling a week rise and for their working week to finish at 1 p.m. on Saturdays. But the strike failed; only some 33 out of 75 men were taken back, at the old rate of wages—13 shillings a week—and for the same hours as before. Despite this setback, Edwards went on to become the founding father of the National Agricultural Workers' Union in 1912.

157 A scene from an agricultural strike, Ashdon, Essex, 1913. The man standing on his head is Frank Barrett, who worked in the brickyard and 'was once a wild man, but was converted at our chapel and became a bold Christian'. Evidently, he was quite a character; for his Sunday best, Barrett wore a suit with pearl buttons and bell-bottom trousers.

159 Lincolnshire Farmers' Union, undated. The Union was set up in 1904 'for the purpose of watching over and defending matters affecting farmers'. No one was eligible as a member unless carrying on the business of a farmer on not less than two acres of land. The first chairman was Edwin Campbell of Stapleford, Newark. By 1907 the union had 40 branches and 3,000 members, and formed the basis of the National Farmers' Union, established in 1908.

160 Tithe distraint sale at Mr C. C. Sanders' farm at Standlake, Oxfordshire, April 1935. Farmers bitterly resented the payment of tithes (fixed as a rent charge) to the Church at a time when, in the early 1930s, the industry was severely depressed. Many refused to pay and attempts by auctioneers to sell farmers' goods for arrears of tithes often led to pitched battles with the authorities. On this occasion over 40 police were present, but failed to prevent the burning of an effigy of Queen Anne; during her reign tithes became part of the Church's revenue known as Queen Anne's Bounty.

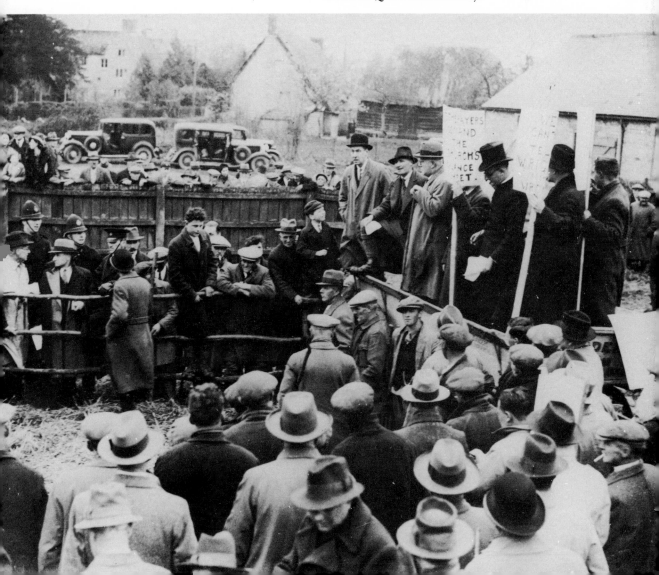

The Great War

161 Troop of Royal Artillery at Ivinghoe, Bucks, leaving for France, 1916.

162 Ladies' sewing meeting to make bandages, outside the Assembly Rooms, Twyford, Berkshire.

163 Wounded soldiers, in their blues, at Sulham Rectory, Berkshire, *c.* 1917. Those in front have been identified as, left to right, Jones, Rutland and Jenkins; the man behind seems to have taken up duties as a chauffeur.

164 Bob Handley being trained for the Friends' Ambulance Unit, at Jordans, Bucks, 1916. As conscientious objectors, many Quakers were unable to fight, serving instead with medical units in the front line. What happened to Bob Handley is unknown, but in this photograph he is seen with Eva Wells, who was responsible for the catering at Jordans (an early Quaker meeting house, near Beaconsfield and the burial place of William Penn).

165 Phyliss Fenner, Women's Land Army. When war broke out, Phyliss's brothers enlisted and she applied to be a nurse, at $13\frac{1}{2}$ years old. In April 1917 she went to a concert with her parents and heard the song 'to be a farmer's boy'; shortly after she joined the WLA, still two years under age. Her initial posting was on a farm in Canterbury, where she looked after the crops, starting work every morning at 7 a.m. Phyliss recalled that when the farmer first left her with the plough she thought 'what do I do when I get to the end of the field? But the horse knew—he turned around'. Later she took a course at Wye College, Kent, which qualified her to work as a supervisor at a vegetable drying factory and when still only 17 she helped manage a Government fruit-pulping factory employing over 100 women.

166 German prisoners helping with the hay harvest, Herefordshire, 1918. The acute shortage of labour to bring in the wartime harvests resulted not only in the employment of women on the land, but also prisoners of war. They were used especially at the end of the war, when in 1918 some 30,000 were employed. Many prisoners were already familiar with farm work and were often preferred to land girls, particularly for the heavier or more disagreeable tasks.

167 The shortage of foodstuffs, made acute by the success of the German U-boat campaigns, led both to an increase in the cultivated area, and to a Government appeal to consume less food. Car stickers such as the one shown here may have been patriotic, but were resented by poorer people actually existing near the 'bread-line'. A Wilder photograph taken in 1917.

168 On their return from war, many were disillusioned
with the 'land fit for heroes' and even for the physically
unharmed, the moral ills of unemployment and
hopelessness all too often awaited. This photograph titled
only 'ex-sailor' tells its own story. Taken by Miss
M. Wight in Herefordshire.

Change in the Countryside

169 Picturesque cottages, Cherhill, Wiltshire, 1930s. The beauty of the English village was an asset almost taken for granted for hundreds of years. Despite the fact that old cottages could be dark and insanitary, their external appearance was often in harmony with their surroundings, being built here of local material in a local tradition. Photograph by Eric Guy.

170 *Opposite above* The interwar period saw enormous change in the physical appearance of the village, as it became, in many areas, less the place where the rural worker lived and more the abode of the urban commuter. Council housing sprang up on the edges of villages, offering better internal accommodation and amenities than the older cottages, but often presenting a rather raw and monotonous aspect. Here at Anstey, in the Charnwood forest area, the building line has been carried too near to the road and a row of elms felled to improve visibility. Taken in the 1930s.

172 Ornate, pretentious villa in a rural setting in Lancashire, probably late 1920s.

171 In the eyes of at least one critic, Clough Williams-Ellis, council housing was still superior to the 'artistic' bungalow or 'country home in the Jacobean style' built to accommodate the new middle-class demand for rural homes, away from the noise and the grime of the city. The bungalows shown in this photograph, at Devoran in Cornwall in the early 1930s, are typical examples of infilling between two existing properties.

174 The growth of private car ownership also brought changes to the countryside. Clough Williams-Ellis noted that those country dwellers who considered themselves safe from the ugliness of the town were 'fools living in a fools' paradise', since 'that comfortable if guilty security has been shattered and exploded by petrol in a million obedient engines'. The photograph shows a petrol station, made of corrugated iron, near Kenilworth, Warwickshire in the late 1920s.

173 Besides being a place of residence, the countryside became a place for leisure. This photograph, taken in London, highlights advertisements by the Great Western Railway for Newton Abbot, 'gateway to Dartmoor' and the 'ideal holiday centre for glorious Devon', as well as those by the London, Midland and Scottish railway for weekend excursions to a variety of destinations.

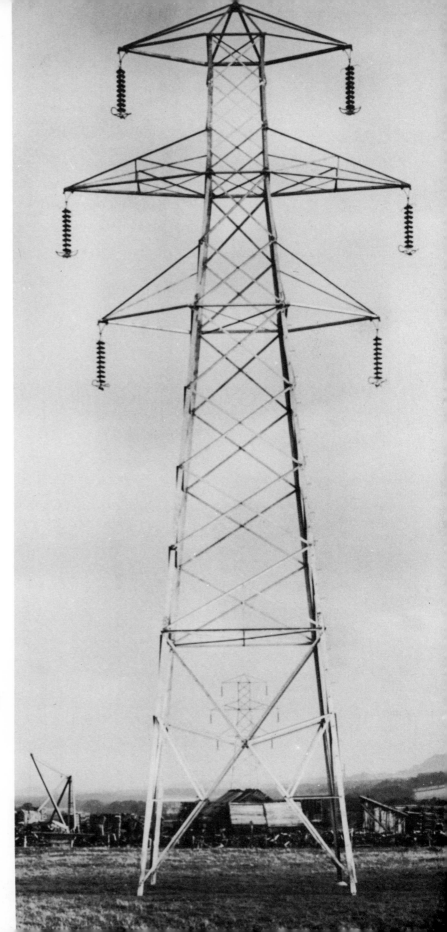

175 *Opposite* Roadside advertising, Wigston, Leicestershire, early 1930s. As the number of road users multiplied, so too did the number of bill posters and advertisement hoardings. When new, such posters might add colour and interest to an otherwise dreary wall, but when tattered, as here, they were a disfigurement. County Councils had certain powers to remove them, but these were rarely exercised.

176 *Opposite below* A particularly strident field sign, late 1920s.

177 Electricity towers in the process of being strung, October 1928. The national grid brought electricity into the villages in the 1930s and contributed a new feature to the landscape. While there is a pleasing beauty in the pylons depicted here, a host of masts and wires could mar an otherwise unspoilt piece of countryside.

The Council for the Preservation of Rural England
was set up in 1926 to keep all such land use changes
under surveillance, to co-ordinate protest and to seek
legislation which would control development in
country areas. The two photographs illustrate what
the CPRE considered to be successful examples of
rural planning.

178 Undereaves electricity. Here an unsightly array of wires, bringing the new supply to this Lancashire village, has been avoided, and a tidy appearance maintained. Taken in the early 1930s.

179 Fitness for purpose. Askers Road House and garage, near Bridport, Dorset, late 1920s. The building was considered to 'imitate nothing, yet achieve real beauty of line'.

Country People Between the Wars

180 A farming family. The photograph shows John Watts Ward, with his wife Mabel and children John Kingdon and Sadie. It was taken at Westdown, a 200-acre farm at Sandy Bay, Littleham near Exmouth, Devon, shortly after they went to live there in March 1928. John Ward changed farms several times in the interwar period in an attempt to make agriculture profitable during the depression years.

181 Gunstone House. The Ward family first farmed at Gunstone, near Yeoford, Crediton, in 1920 but left there about four years later. John Ward did not sell the farm, however, preferring to lease it out to a family called Soper. He and his wife returned in 1937, and remained until their retirement.

182 John Kingdon Ward (on left) 1936. The son did not go into farming, but opted instead to become a surveyor, working in London and Lancashire before the outbreak of war. He is seen here with a chainman, surveying the route for a new arterial road, at Chorley, Lancashire.

183 Rural workers, at Leavenheath, Suffolk, summer 1935. Shown from left to right are 'Turner', an ex-farm labourer; Bill Petch, lodger and pigman at Leaden Hall farm; Billy Holder, householder and agricultural contractor; Muriel Holder, his wife; Maria Darnell, a family friend, and her sister and brother-in-law. The cottage, brick-built with a slated roof, was originally a double-dwelling, comprising two large rooms downstairs with hall, larder and lean-to kitchen with an oil stove for cooking. Upstairs were two large bedrooms and a smaller room. Water was drawn from a well about 100 yards away. There was a pit-type privy in the garden and a rainwater butt outside the back door. The floors were dirt with bricks, laid on edge. They were covered with a thick layer of newspapers and linoleum laid on top, an arrangement common in Suffolk cottages at this time.

184 Many farmworkers left the land altogether in the interwar period, hoping for a better life in the towns. This photograph shows one such family, no longer young, on the road, with their pets and scanty possessions. A Miss M. Wight photograph, taken in Herefordshire in 1939.

185 Theodore Lamb, Sibford Gower, Oxfordshire, 1930s. Some country people were unable to find a permanent niche in life, becoming local characters and even attracting the attention of the press. Theodore was one such. He was born about 1880 in Sibford, attended a local Quaker school and was later apprenticed to a watchmaker in Banbury. He became a skilled watch- and clock-mender. But when called up in the First World War, he went to Oxford for his interview, said not a word and was sent home again. He lived the last 40 years of his life as a hermit in a shack on Sibford heath. He would travel round, sometimes on a bicycle without tyres, sometimes on foot, and usually with some form of truck loaded with junk and, in the winter, with his fire in a bucket as well. He made a whistle out of a piece of bicycle frame, on which he would play to collect money. He always paid for his small needs, although when his clothing, which was often made of sacks, became less than decent he was banned from Banbury and had to wait at the door of the village shop to be served. He was always totally honest and completely harmless and in later life coachloads of sightseers from Birmingham and neighbouring towns would stop to see Theodore and perhaps get a photograph, if they paid him sufficiently well for the privilege. He died in March 1950, having been found collapsed by the roadside a few days previously. He had saved sufficient money to pay for his funeral, which was held at the Friends' Meeting House and was well attended.

The Coming of World War Two

186 Devon farmers' mounted and armed with service rifles, have formed the first cavalry troop of the Home Guard. They patrolled in a giant ring around Exmoor as a guard against German parachutists. From dawn to dusk they maintained a constant watch, working in relays during the harvest period. Photograph taken in August 1940.

FESTIVALS OF THE WORLD
IRELAND

W

FRANKLIN WATTS
LONDON•SYDNEY

This edition first published in 2006 by
Franklin Watts
338 Euston Road
London
NW1 3BH

This edition is published for sale only in the United
Kingdom & Eire.

© Marshall Cavendish International (Asia) Pte Ltd 2006
Originated and designed by Marshall Cavendish
International (Asia) Pte Ltd
A member of Times Publishing Limited
Times Centre, 1 New Industrial Road
Singapore 536196

Written by: Patricia McKay
Edited by: Katharine Brown-Carpenter
Designed by: Agnes Lim
Picture research: Thomas Khoo and Joshua Ang

A CIP catalogue record for this book is available from
the British Library.

ISBN 0 7496 6775 3

Dewey Classification: 394.269417

Printed in Malaysia

CONTENTS